You and Me

Now It's Your Turn

Denise M. Jordan

Heinemann Library
Chicago, Illinois

Designed by Sue Emerson, Heinemann Library; Page layout by Que-Net Media™
Printed and bound in China by South China Printing Company Limited
Photo research by Janet Lankford Moran

08 07 06 05 04
10 9 8 7 6 5 4 3 2 1

Library of Congress Cataloging-in-Publication Data
Jordan, Denise.
    Now it's your turn / Denise M. Jordan.
        p. cm. – (You and me)
Summary: Simple text and pictures explain how, why, where, and when we take turns.
    ISBN 1-4034-4405-6 (HC), 1-4034-4411-0 (Pbk.)
    1. Sharing–Juvenile literature. [1. Sharing.] I. Title.
    BJ1533.G4J67 2003
    177'.1–dc22

                                        2003012819

Acknowledgments
The author and publishers are grateful to the following for permission to reproduce copyright material:
pp. 4, 5, 7, 13, 18, 19, 21 Warling Studios/Heinemann Library; pp. 6, 8, 15, 16, 17, 20 Que-Net/Heinemann Library; p. 9 Jose Luis Pelaez, Inc./Corbis; p. 10 Myrleen Ferguson Cate/PhotoEdit Inc.; p. 11 Mary Kate Denny/PhotoEdit Inc.; p. 12 Ted Horowitz/Corbis; p. 14 Ariel Skelley/Corbis; pp. 22, 24 Janet L. Moran/Oijoy Photography; p. 23 (T-B) Warling Studios/Heinemann Library, Mary Kate Denny/PhotoEdit Inc., Janet L. Moran/Oijoy Photography; back cover (L-R) Warling Studios/Heinemann Library, Janet L. Moran/Oijoy Photography

Cover photograph by Warling Studios/Heinemann Library

Every effort has been made to contact copyright holders of any material reproduced in this book. Any omissions will be rectified in subsequent printings if notice is given to the publisher.

Special thanks to our advisory panel for their help in the preparation of this book:
Alice Bethke, Library Consultant
Palo Alto, CA

Eileen Day, Preschool Teacher
Chicago, IL

Kathleen Gilbert,
Second Grade Teacher
Round Rock, TX

Sandra Gilbert,
Library Media Specialist
Fiest Elementary School
Houston, TX

Jan Gobeille,
Kindergarten Teacher
Garfield Elementary
Oakland, CA

Angela Leeper,
Educational Consultant
Wake Forest, NC

Some words are shown in bold, **like this.**
You can find them in the picture glossary on page 23.

Contents

What Is Taking Turns?

Taking turns means sharing with others.

Sharing means some for you and some for me.

I get a turn.

Now, it's your turn.

We can use it together.

Where Can You Take Turns?

You can take turns at home.

You can take turns using the **sink** to wash your hands.

You can take turns on the school playground, too.

Everyone can have a turn!

Why Do You Take Turns?

You take turns because you want to share with others.

When you share you can make someone happy.

You take turns when you want
to help, too!

Helping others is a good thing
to do.

Who Can You Take Turns With?

You can take turns with your family.

You can take turns during dinnertime.

You can take turns with your classmates.

You can take turns drinking water from the water **fountain.**

What Do You See When You Take Turns?

You can see people sharing what they have with others.

They can make something together.

You can see people having fun.

Everyone can play together!

What Do You Hear When You Take Turns?

You may hear someone ask, "May I have a turn?"

You might say, "Now, it's your turn."

You also hear words like "please" and "thank you."

How Can You Take Turns at Home?

You can take turns helping at home.

Today, you can help your mom with the dishes.

Tomorrow, your sister will help.

Now, it is your turn again!

How Can You Take Turns at School?

You can take turns during music time.

You can play the **bongos** first.

Later, your classmate can play the bongos.

You are sharing when you take turns.

How Do You Feel When You Take Turns?

You can feel happy when you take turns.

When you take turns with others, they are happy, too!

Taking turns can make you smile!

It feels good when you take turns.

Quiz

How can you take turns?

Look for the answer on page 24.

Picture Glossary

bongos
pages 18, 19

fountain
page 11

sink
page 6

Note to Parents and Teachers

Reading for information is an important part of a child's literacy development. Learning begins with a question about something. Help children think of themselves as investigators and researchers by encouraging their questions about the world around them. Each chapter in this book begins with a question. Read the question together. Look at the pictures. Talk about what you think the answer might be. Then read the text to find out if your predictions were correct. Think of other questions you could ask about the topic, and discuss where you might find the answers.

Index

Answer to quiz on page 22

You can have a turn.
Now, she can have a turn.